Two Runs Alon

Also by Rodney Williams and published by Ginninderra Press

A Bird-loving Man

In This Dusty Rear-view Mirror

Love Showing Here Now (Pocket Poets)

Two Runs Alongside the Island

Twenty-five poems

Rodney Williams

Acknowledgements

Part of this collection appeared in *Love Showing Here Now* (GP Pocket Poets 102, series editor Brenda Eldridge, 2019). One other poem (modified here) was first included in an anthology also produced by Ginninderra Press: *I Protest – Poems of Dissent* (ed. Stephen Matthews, 2020). Further poetry was initially published in: *The Adelaide Literary Magazine* (NYC) & *Antipodes* (also USA); *Page Seventeen, Right Now & StylusLit* (Aust); another piece will also appear in *Brushstrokes II – 2020/ 21 Ros Spencer Poetry Contest Anthology* (WA Poets) later in 2021.

In memory of Garry O'Shannassy, for joining me – fifty years ago – in writing first poems, no matter how modest; OSha, you've been taken since, much too soon…

With loving gratitude to Meg Long, for all her breadth of reading and depth of thinking, her inspiration and care, across more than forty years.

And special appreciation for support received from Stephen Matthews & Brenda Eldridge at Ginninderra Press, over various projects in recent times.

Along with deep respect for the work of P.D. Gardner & Annemieke Mein, as well as the keepers of the Krowathunkooloong Keeping Place, Bairnsdale, East Gippsland, Victoria.

Two Runs Alongside the Island: twenty-five poems
ISBN 978 1 76109 195 7

Cover image: Rodney Williams

First published 2021 by
GINNINDERRA PRESS
PO Box 3461 Port Adelaide 5015
www.ginninderrapress.com.au

Contents

Foreword

Exploring issues like the need to respect a fragile environment and the rights of marginalised people (with quite a focus placed on migration), this collection is underpinned by the belief we should show greater care for fellow humans; for our world; for other living things. I wrote 'All too readily' in February 2020 for Ginninderra Press's *I Protest* anthology, before Black Lives Matter protests in mid-year also objected to monuments honouring people infamous for racism. True to its title, across *Two Runs Alongside the Island: twenty-five poems* you might identify dual perspectives on some questions. May a sense of empathy towards others shine through in this work, along with an eye for place; an impulse to reflect; a drive to create; a thirst to be.

The last piece you will find here was the final one to be written. Sixty-five years old now, I can only smile in looking back at early efforts to write poems when aged fifteen. I had more luck then in building a bookcase: it is the one substantial physical possession to have stayed with me across a full half-century. Like my poetry writing, it celebrates its golden anniversary here.

For some time now, traditional Western poetic forms have compelled me in particular, due to their shape, their echoes, their demands, their elegance. Whether sestinas, sonnets, triolets or villanelles, the requirements prescribed by set structures can be enabling as well as limiting, prompting inventiveness. I relish experimenting with various approaches, weaving a range of textures: devising my own frameworks, using syllabic patterns, as in the micropoem 'Sign'. Revering vers libre, of course, for the very freedom which it offers, I constantly test an ear for cadence, aspiring towards musicality of language. You will find me attracted by natural settings, historical contexts and numerical metaphors. Despite writing digitally, I still scribble potential phrases onto scraps of paper in the middle of the night, fearful of losing fleeting images that might become effective. Perhaps they will have an emotive impact. They could feel vivid or immediate, appealing to the senses. They may be thought-provoking as ideas, suggestive in symbolism. Whether this work achieves such heights is up to you to determine.

All poems selected here have been written in recent times. True to fifty years of learning from a rotating set of volumes housed in one old bookcase, this book hopes to pay testament to a life spent pursuing what Dylan Thomas – a hero of my youth – called this 'craft and sullen art'…

Rodney Williams

Part 1

Poems About Environments & Animals

Texts From a Twin Gulfs Road trip

Gulf St Vincent – Spencer Gulf, South Australia

I

grazing rights defined by strands of barbed wire
over this barest of claypans
on land never fenced
by first owners
with sheep nibbling a living from saltbush nearby
renowned for producing the tastiest lamb –
settlers' stonewalls propped upright by braces
long since not offering any roof
to a conscience

II

white pipes through golden canola on the right
drawing water from rains way up north
pumped out of that arterial river
towards the steel city at the head of these gulfs –
wind turbines on the ridge to the left
slowly rolling
their cartwheels relentlessly
anticlockwise

III

a crop-duster aircraft
directed by GPS
banking hard to turn for another run
swooping in low to unload
across bread-basket fields
lush with lentils

IV

a desert mindset premature
at that golf course alongside the road
with putting greens turned black as asphalt
from engine oil spilt across sand scrapes
despite fields in every direction
made verdant by spring irrigation

V

pademelon fruit abundant
on either edge of this highway
among legacies left by Afghan cameleers
through seeds dropped at random
from saddles with splitting seams

VI

a thin lip of silver sea
glinting in afternoon glare to the west –
to the east a backdrop of ranges
named for an explorer
first to pilot white
sails around the whole rim
of this breakaway landmass
long owned in spirit by others

VII

capturing sunlight in a myriad of mirrors
at the top of a tower so tall
clear as a coastal beacon
growing truss tomatoes en masse
for markets overseas
with its miracles extending
to condensing fresh water from salt

VIII

in this most northerly port
at the head of the gulf country
the world's largest lead smelter
for more than a century
(still a claim to fame
worth boasting about
it seems)
loading up for export
beside wheat and barley
certified as toxin-free

IX

beyond yet another stretch
of pipeline across these plains
a vintage automobile
for decades abandoned
corroding in country so dry
ferrous red as any gibber stone
its rusted bonnet raised
like fingertips touching
extended in supplication
for some deeper accord
still to be answered

After the buy-back

Australian Wildlife Conservancy, Kalamurina, SA

a mound of sand
the width of a wombat
held firmly in place once more
by the roots of a spindly shrub returning
to the hardest of baked-flat claypans
swept bare long before this dry
by those parching winds of drought
with no soil beyond that creek's green edge
after heavy-hooved intruders
had overgrazed this station
till rounded up in their last muster
meaning now this hummock is home again
to such a native marsupial
ever so small in human hands
its own return here a triumph
with its tiny teeth razor-sharp
free to emerge from a tunnelled lair
under cover of desert darkness
leaving only the lightest of paw prints
its larder tail trailing behind
when preying on fellow sand dwellers
suited in size to this dunnart
across a ribcage of parallel dunes
out in so vast a continent's centre

fearsome as any feral feline
much less a home-ground dingo
gram for gram
when not forced to fight
much too far above
its own featherweight division

In a cage

Fraser Island, Queensland

on docking at the jetty we spot that fence first up
a compound to keep folk safe, it emerges
obliging us to swap roles with wildlife for once
protecting ourselves in a cage by reversal

with this dingo pack pure in its genes – isolated –
mainlanders pose the biggest threat of all:
prone to visit the island at night by boat
laying poisoned baits by stealth from offshore

once we dare to venture outside the wire
we spot scarlet honeyeaters – a lifetime first:
their plumage bright red as blood from a cut
after we'd failed at other attempts heretofore

from there we pass by a barrage lake
closed since dingoes took meat from a child
only to bite another in demanding more
leaving them fed by a ranger's gun instead

off Indian Head at the east edge of this island –
the largest in the world made out of sand,
held by a volcano against the ocean –
manta rays roll on swells from the Andes

whether a fever or squadron this set of great rays
clocks currents, wind-shifts, off-shore squalls
keeping watch over the tidal suck of the moon
confronting the Pacific for the sake of us all

we miss our chance for a last glimpse of dingoes
their signature paw prints scribed in sand
between tide lines twixt high and low water
in a blink beneath this pier at dawn

in lockdown later as a result of this virus
keeping our distance (as required)
we stay safe back home down south – isolated –
protecting ourselves in a cage once more

Multimedia whale watch

Albany, Western Australia

no one's commencing here by commanding
that you should call him Ishmael
self-styled as a novel's narrator
as sole surviving ship's crew member
if once a biblically exiled outcast
holding on hard to so much text since
not simply some piece of flotsam
so as to tell a tale of his skipper Ahab
and that white-whale compulsion

this is no video of a Nantucket sleighride
dragged by ropes behind a whaleboat
with harpoon barbs still embedded
nor any digital animation on podcast
of a cautionary scriptural parable
depicting a sinner duly condemned
to spend three days in a whale's gullet
before being coughed back up repentant
a myth also at home in comic books

right now no song sung by a blue whale
can be heard streaming online either
lilting and yearning while it is shifting
in pitch spanning that baritone register
from the biggest of possible soundboxes
with so ghostly a grief-filled resonance
mourning New England's tides of blood
all the way down to Cape Leeuwin's lighthouse
with no network where oceans meet

without room for my copy of *Whale Nation*
in this mobile library (verse graphic as colour
photos showing blades and blood in flensing)
I write postcards as a drive-by whale-spotter
with these old binos plus a telephoto lens
far too small to have strong enough zooms
from windswept clifftops and rocky outcrops
coastal installations and viewing platforms
making potential sightings speculation

never one for wine-and-whales TV travelogues
from Margaret River along a dream coast
but with too much data for Instagram postings
I search for a blog of real time spottings
where my co-driver could post her screenshots
once that distant sliver dark in shape
shows itself as neither rock nor reef
spouting as it swims across the horizon
although there's no humpback breaching

we check in at the museum in Albany
behind a Moby Dick white tour bus
disgorging a belly full of Jonahs
into a cinema's virtual whaling montage
showing historic black-and-white footage
complete with an Ishmael commentary
whereas we see a southern right whale instead
– always the best one, true to its name –
rising in the harbour in real time, live and free

Looking for signs at Koala Corner

Uralla Nature Reserve, Trafalgar, Victoria
for Jai

where these three paths all meet
each plainly labelled on signage
here at the top of Bullocky Track
in this old-growth bushland reserve
an interpretive panel honours
not bullock drivers but timber fellers
captured in sepia across a century
on planks they knew as spring boards
after their axes had chopped out notches
for their latest makeshift ladder
on either side of an upright trunk
their crosscut saw between them…
yet no signs remain here otherwise
of stumps from mountain grey gums
such men left behind as remnants
to rot away deep-rooted

on a morning remaining overcast
down that slope in the western quarter
the loud chatter of a lyrebird
mimics other forest dwellers
not least a two-toned whip-crack call
picked up from an eastern whipbird –
both birds well known as evasive
despite remaining within earshot –
yet no sightings can be made today
beyond these random scratchings
left here in scattered leaf-litter
still moist from overnight rain

there's no glimpse to boast of either
with the elusive Strzelecki koala
famed for feeding that explorer
a creature listed as being at-risk now
although claimed to be a regular
renowned for visiting this corner
in truth never seen at these crossroads
regardless of naming-right honours

bushwalkers debate what they could rightly see
themselves as forgiving God for
yet there's still no sign to spot from the heavens
except those darker storm clouds

Two runs alongside the island

San Remo, Victoria

1.

above the gleam
of that bay to the north
blanched silver by sunlight
driving along this motorcyclist's route
towards the Grand Prix racetrack
bound for the bridge
to Phillip Island
I spot a rufous fox on our right
at full pace in rich pasture
being chased
by a pair of ravens
diving in darkly
against shoulder and head

2.

boarding this ferry
thanks to you my love
set to trace the coast south to the cape
past a pair of fur seals
raising flippers in prayer
beyond cliffs of granite
turned verdant by run-off
I ride that thumping swell
my arms clamped tight around the rail
right up at the prow
despite sea salt spraying
on this russet beard turned grey
facing Bass Strait's surge for Father's Day

Part 2

Verses on Human Rights & Marginalised People

Six points for charting William Cuffay

'We are political serfs – we demand to be free. We therefore invite all well disposed to join in our peaceful procession on Monday next, April 10, as it is for the good of all that we seek to remove the evils under which we groan.' Proclamation for a mass meeting of British Chartists, 1848

I

his grandpa was freed from slavery
William Cuffay's father too
as a navy cook from St Kitts
while Will's mother hailed from Kent
where her son got himself stitched
apprenticed to a tailor
till pressed to the first of his furies
at losing such a position
indentures not worth a thimble
once he found himself sacked through striking
for workers' days of three fair shifts
eight hours each to labour, relax and rest

II

those Six Points from Cuffay's Chartists
proclaimed suffrage as inviolate
for any free man sound of mind
on attaining twenty-one years
at elections held each twelve-month
across districts matched in scope
with candidates needing no land to stand
their incomes paid by Treasury
all members free to vote in secret
in keeping with their conscience
yet when the great petitioned protest
massing on Kennington Common
failed to march on Parliament House
in London William was left incensed
with that broadsheet taking the name of the times
deriding this black man and his party

III

convicted of sedition
on the song of one canary
who swore the defendant was complicit
in a plot to burn down buildings
as a sign for imminent uprising
Cuffay was eloquent in his outrage
at a lack of rightful trial
before a jury of worker equals
from that dock to be transported
down to Van Diemen's Land for life
whence a punchy journal threw its low blow
casting Mr C as undertaker
too neglectful to care to close
eyes said to have been left open
on the corpse of the Chartist cause

IV

four-foot eleven-inches tall
small in body if not stature
he was deformed in spine from birth
yet not twisted in his spirit
with skin in plain terms rated dark
so by complexion listed
in Cuffay's convict transcript
if not blackened in his conscience

V

choosing to linger down in Hobart Town
despite exoneration by the Crown
Cuffay thence won a sharp campaign
that forced colonial powers
to cut clauses of punitive temper
from laws for master and servant
in the island's legislature

VI

through to his early eighties
William Cuffay fought a dogged fight
against health as poor as his purse –
while he died a pauper in a workhouse
tributes appeared in three colonies
with his grave-site noted for marking
in the Trinity burying ground
yet folk free to vote in Tasmania
have not since seen fit to honour
with headstone, plaque or statue
that spot where rest the remnants
of this president of Chartists

Sign

Love
showing
here now at
Immigration
Museum
for short
time

Dogs of Australia

For German migrants interned as enemy aliens on Torrens Island in the Port Adelaide River estuary during World War I.

1

I am a dog of Australia
Walked here by this country's first people
Across a land bridge long since flooded
An apex hunter as desert dweller
At home as a loner or part of a pack
I am this country's wild dog
After me a town's called Warragul
But my true name is the dingo
I am a dog of Australia

2

I am a dog of Australia
Striped with ochre on rocks to the north
A marsupial wolf since wiped from this land
Saved by the strait for that isle to the south
Yet bounties on my skull for sheep-kills
Will let me live on only in myth
Known as the Tasmanian tiger
My true name is the thylacine
I am a dog of Australia

3

I am a dog of Australia
As bred by outback cattlemen
Crossing breeds from Britain with dingoes
Renowned as alert and loyal
Herding stock with nips to the achilles
Sharing farm kennels with kelpies
My true name is the Australian cattle dog
Known to most as the Queensland blue heeler
I am a dog of Australia

4

I am a dog of Australia
As bred by German foresters
To hunt badgers, rabbits and foxes
My spirit not skinny like my body down burrows
Yet laughed at down here as a sausage dog
I'm kicked in the belly while held on a leash
Since cruelty's become patriotic
My true name is *der Dachshund*
I am a dog of Australia

5

I am a dog of Australia
Linked in blood to the wolves of Black Forest
Loved as guardian, searcher and guide
My spirit proudest among canines worldwide
Even in war, no one's kicking my ribs
Those footpath patriots not so brave
Known as the Alsatian or German shepherd
My true name is *der deutsche Schäferhund*
I am a dog of Australia

6

I am a dog of Australia
Still linked in blood to my kind in Europe
Punched this far south by iron-mailed fists
A welcome migrant, my skills in demand
Down here these days I'm kicked in the guts
Accused of sabotage against my new home
Interned without cause after years of peace
My true name is *ein Deutsch-Australien*
I am a German Australian

Hedging our bets

'… since I stopped full-time gardening, the petrol-driven leaf-blower…has almost entirely replaced the rake… This book has nothing to do with the leaf-blower.' – Alice Oswald, *The Thunder Mutters – 101 Poems for the Planet* (Faber, 2005)

Planting straight as strings
You used to clip us privets
Sharp-edged on either line
Shouldering into shoulders
As a solid set. Never for us
That expanse of root-earth
Left free around elm trees.
At our best, no open space
Across lawns, as with oaks
Living solo. Hand-trimmed
It was always wisest for us
To pull our heads in closer
In hedging our bets as one:
Rosellas scattered our seed.

Upon our forks nest fellow
Imports, the song thrush &
Blackbird, singing with all
Their hearts for home: like
Us pushed south under sail.
We alone are seen as a pest.
Native trees pose their own
Risks to all forest dwellers:
Eucalypts drip spills of sap
Blood-red on brown trunks
And smooth pink branches.
Once hollowed, their limbs
Offer a nest hole to a parrot,
But a widowmaker to a man.

Ourselves we dare not differ
Since scissored until square,
Wary of that hedge-trimmer
No hedge clippers any more
With thickest stems docked
By a roaring chainsaw now.
Sap-lines dating back to an
Old-growth heritage hedge
Shield us no longer against
Taproots being pulled from
Soil to air, to drown as fish.
In rating us a noxious weed,
Be fair in whom you blame
If using an axe all the same.

Razor wire childhood

before a royal commission
one sketch:
this girl's face
behind bars
her hair and clothes
black
all her tears
from blue eyes
bleeding red

without yuletide
gifts at christmas
island
no matter
the faith
to which she was born
there was just
one present
she'd prayed for

Best of all

People of Aboriginal descent are respectfully advised that this poem contains the name of a deceased person.

as his trainer
calls it in the gym
that's how it goes:
it's jab, jab
and jab again
from Lionel Rose

in a park with installation art
beside a rural railway station
stands this full-sized statue
funded by subscriptions
its profile strong in bronze –
that former boxing champion
from the bantamweight division
leans in with such a forward press
set to throw a big left hand
his title undisputed
the belt around his midriff
the first won by his people

way over there in Tokyo
more than fifty years ago
our young Indigenous challenger
let rip with combinations
jabs and feints and crosses
crisp as any boxer
knocking down the titleholder
in a flurry on the ropes –
fight-fan locals there at ringside
could only nod, conceding
this kid was loosing left hooks
so sharp they shook the world

as the commentator
calls the fight
that's how it goes:
it's jab, jab
and jab again
from Lionel Rose

reared in a one-room tin shed
right out there on Jackson's Track
until the age of ten,
this Koorie youngster of nineteen
outboxed the Japanese champion
nicknamed Fighting Harada
befitting his brawling style –
while a third judge rated the bout a draw
both the other adjudicators
gave this Australian kid the world crown
even in nineteen-sixty-eight
no home bias in their scores

returning here to massive plaudits
Lionel thought that airport crowd
must have been there for the Beatles...
although later pressed for cash himself
he gave heart to young men jailed:
after all the push and pull of fame
he was granted a state funeral –
back at that statue beside the train track
a lone bloom left up in his left glove
put there by some late-night lover
was still a rose for our Rose
such small tokens best of all

in black-and-white
as I recall
that's how it goes:
it's jab, jab
and jab again
from Lionel Rose

All too readily

Councillors with a mandate to govern East Gippsland,
you will be aware the Electoral Commission
has altered the title of McMillan – ever a swinging seat –
in response to a groundswell of grief, federal in its reach.

You should be all too painfully conscious in conscience
that you now sit stalled yourselves at a crossroad,
once you consult a map charting regional memorials
honouring a pioneer still renowned with naming-rights
on street signs and monuments by rivers and lakes,
despite all too readily spilling blood onto water.

You will be acutely cognisant how much – worldwide –
voices passionate in their protest have pushed back hard
against a history of atrocity still atrophied in bronze.

Remember yourselves how a cairn on the Dargo Road –
beside a creek misnamed as Iguana, surely Goanna –
commemorates the spot where this Scotsman met his demise,
boasting his side-whiskers and signature tam o' shanter,
only to see his cheekbone (its cast tarnished) meet a blow
from hammer onto punch – as hollow as a bullet-hole –
having died penniless, despite all the country he stole.

Take care not to condone his band of Caledonian horsemen –
a Highland Brigade – having fired muskets as they charged
through families shucking shells at firesides by a creek;
leaving him to sample skulls as souvenirs in his saddlebags,
after all too readily spilling blood into water.

Part 3

Lines From Relationships

Peering across to the other side

short fiction in verse

Peering across to the other side
of this post-and-rail fence
bordering our first-ever rented backyard
you offer your myopic squint
as yet to put your contacts in
gorgeous even when bleary-eyed
but rising from bed as well myself
I feel no better focused
on the mistiest morning so far this spring
with my glasses fogging up instantly
despite my curiosity
about progress in the garage next door
with that retro roadster set on blocks
just a blur in racing red.

As one we transfer our attention
to garden plots against this boundary fence
much loved by a woman
still sorely missed
her prized flower beds
overgrown with weeds
turned gold by buttercups
more than daffodils now.

Yet our focal point this morning must be
that cobwebbed henhouse next door
which we have offered
to clear if we can share
a hatchery used only by spiders these days.

Just uphill from that linking gate
padlocked without sign of a key
we catch a glimpse
of the old boy himself
our landlord-neighbour –
catch him out, red-handed, in fact.

Long-sighted enough
to be shifting his gaze
from side to side
trusting a blind eye
will surely be turned
he stretches over the railing regardless
his fingers aquiver
as he snips for himself
the best of our bearded iris blooms
so tall and distinct
with their handsome stems
fulsome as burgundy
wine in their petals
their leaves as purple
as capillaries bruised.

Forever his late love's
favourite flowers
we've grown them from rhizomes
she'd thinned out herself.

He forced them on us
as a house-warming gift
unwelcome at first
last autumn
back then just a nuisance in our eyes
in contrast to how we have since
come to see
such a lonely old age as his…

Sonnet from Sophie's wedding

for Meg

In need of no bridesmaid, our daughter –
true to herself in how she would marry;
true to her love – asked you her mother
to be at her side before that mirror:
later at the reception your speech
was aquiver in hand and voice alike,
courageous in your terror as much
as candid about truths held close for life.
Three and a half decades shared as such
had not sparked disclosures from you my wife
as held family and guests that night in thrall:
vulnerability in marriage – which
you extolled – left others moist of eye,
disarming me, sweet darling, most of all.

A pair of number-seven flat irons

a figure any soul pressed to service
could only dread to gaze down at
across every seven days of work
that number standing out starkly
from such a foundry casting
right here beneath this handle

now owning a pair of twin pressers
lets me toil away all the harder
but it's still my older flat iron
which smooths out rumples the best
in this kitchen misty with steam
full of garments hung here for privilege
no dress-up games permitted
yet two miniatures made for youngsters
played with as irons by girls around my feet
as river boats by those boys

with my best number-seven at rest now
still too warm for a toy on its trivet
bought to block scorch marks on this oak bench
more shielded as timber than skin
this second flat iron glows hot on the hob
till I lift it with care from the stovetop
sharp-nosed from its molten moulding
shaped to work around buttons on dresses
bagged up in burlap from our betters

some folk still call these sad irons
with such a label thought to have lingered
from a long-lapsed old-world coining
said to stand for being solid or heavy
true to both this pair of flat irons
weighty blocks against scarred fingers
fierce with heat that flattens creases
in prime cotton from the gentry
for all my pains well pressed

seven
pounds in each of these sad irons
seven
burns across my chapped hands
seven
more skirts and pinafores to press
seven
nights till he comes back home again
seven
times he'll try to push hot himself
seven
bairns not just mine now my sister's too
seven
months till they will number
eight
except if once more it's twins

Place value

a maths teacher's break-up poem – for Liz

what's shifting
positions
for us
between
unite
&
untie
is
i
if not
u
that's us now
to a
t

Part 4

Stanzas For Travellers

You wonder if you're in trouble when

What are we waiting for all crowded in the forum?
The Barbarians are to arrive today.
– C. P. Cavafy (trans. John Mavrogordato, Hogarth, 1971)

Southern Cross Railway Station, Melbourne, Victoria

you wonder if you're in trouble when
the control crew at this train station
programs those escalators on either side
each to descend at once against you
such that your only escape from down here
will be to clamber up top breathless
via the staircase in the centre
despite the threat of a missed connection
over that overarching concourse
above this steel-grind metro platform
where you've alighted in a crush-rush

you catch it's not all calm on the catwalk
when you spot a face pale with anaemia
above a T-shirt from a merch stall
white text blazed across black fabric
starkly labelled *UFC*
which prompts you then to speculate
if this boy has been to a soccer match
in support of a *united football club*
of which you've never heard
only to sigh at all that eludes you
after thumbing over your mobile
to learn instead he's just been watching the
ultimate fighting championship

you fear you're in a spot of bother when
you find yourself in the charge-path
of a best-of-the-rest tsunami
making its exit from that stadium
while some squad of twitchy constables
has been detailed to act as lifeguards
directing swimmers between the flags
despite no arms raised in peril
as waves break with feints and parries
threatening in their tide rip
after the victor's kicks and chops and punches
had registered sub-oceanic
on concussion's richter scale
stopping that title fight dead with a tremor
in only its second round

you know you're really in a predicament when
men with thoughts on who just fought
as crowded as their tattoo sleeves
flanked by women languid in blinking
eyelash extensions dark as kohl
all descend from that colosseum
to catch this outbound bullet ship
their swell converting the calm of your capsule
to a pugilistic chatroom
reliving a fight staged in a wire cage
wherein *ultimate* should have read *unlimited*
in terms of blows permissible
beyond the marquess' traditional rules
while a guffaw applauds the champion
for throwing some real sharp elbows
as your phone links you back to a forum
where citizens sit in wait for barbarians

Two or three storeys tall

a triolet

two or three storeys tall
the old stone buildings lean
in close to hear travellers' tales
two or three stories tall
enough to shock one and all
in this cobbled streetscape scene
two or three storeys tall
the old stone buildings lean

Tour guide at the Getty

Los Angeles, California

so next we turn to Rembrandt
whose *Old Man in Military Costume*
is crowned by a plume of ostrich
brash for battlefield headgear
despite a sombre palette of browns
above a riveted martial breastplate
gleaming as burnished steel

a limpid spill of light slants down
over this old boy's listening ear
divided brow
and wispy beard
across his lunar septum
casting a half-moon into shadow
with youth long since eclipsed

by every reckoning
past his fighting best
he is still kitted up for battle
his moist green eyes askance
left of centre in their focus
oblique in reflecting
all of our ageing…

Part 5

Songs of Creativity, Ageing & Self

Beginning with a given line

from Naomi

taking a break from a paintbrush
having a rest from haiku
putting poetry
and prose
paragraphs
and parallels
on hold
finding a gap
between lines
formed by pen
and pencil
pastel
and print
to let the lungs
of my fancy
my love
for balance
between abstractions
my penchant
for distractions
within a moment
take a big deep breath
and sigh

Red parrot

youth
is a bright
red parrot
that dips
at risk
yet rises
against the pressure
of thin blue
air
its calls
both clicking
and chiming
on the wing
first as greeting
then in warning
across
the swell
of grassland
swerving
to alight
in a gum tree
claiming sanctuary
in a rotted
hollow
where it makes
a nest
and lays

Memory

a sestina

memory can fail as a camera for time
leaving portfolios bare
except for snapshot moments
so sharp as to last
in our mind's eye the longest
not printed as the proofs we'd pledged to post across

on those worst of days, our minds might not span across
every priority competing for time
making working life too tense to bear
without a few free moments
to relax at last
until we recall that commitment we had dreaded the longest

shows of legerdemain from folk who live longest
make caring a cross
when elderly conjurors play tricks with time –
they shuffle facts under cups, then lay them bare
in moist-eyed moments
fooling only themselves right through to the last

debits and credits, first to last
we keep our books balanced the longest
we can, sliding beads of recollection across
that abacus which sums up time
even if audits grow too fraught to bear
in our own accounts of deficit moments

at unforeseen moments
we shudder at failures that outlast
our successes, when those longest
claws of regret make scratches across
scars which had healed over time
reopening old wounds all too blood-bare

bare
moments
last
longest
across
time

it's the ache in that tune which lasts the longest –
across decades in time – as an echo
from moments when love first laid us bare

If I had to go

an aria – for Meg

if I had to go
all of a sudden,
caught by surprise
before my projected time,
prior to taking all those chances
I couldn't quite grasp,
singing all these sad songs
I should never have sung
along with
out of tune,
not valuing in full all those folk
I should have acknowledged far more
face to face,
I'd also want to have said
the most heartfelt of thanks,
not only to you –
my darling who mends me –
but to a whole chorale of singers,
beginning with robert johnson
for a delta full of blues,
shining two lights on behind
for mick jagger and keith richards
with love in vain,
whereas eric clapton's layla
has always got me on my knees, either way –
john lennon as well, with his plea
to give peace a chance, despite a warm gun,
leaving stephen stills to warn

there's something happening here
for what it's worth,
as ominous as joe strummer's pulse beat
with war declared
in london calling,
an atlantic blockade away
from lou reed's new york city cool
and his three chords played real good
through sweet jane,
just as patti smith washes her hands
of someone's sins
but not hers
with gloria,
in sync with edith piaf back in paris
having regretted nothing either,
whereas emmylou harris
rocks her soul for her lost gram
from boulder to birmingham…
meanwhile back closer to home
nick cave remains hypnotic as ever
in making that primordial call
to come loose your dogs upon him
in the ship song,
as tom waits waltzes our own matilda
at a smoky piano bar offshore
in tom traubert's blues…
prompting a swing in the axis
of this planet,
bringing a shift in key to match
minor in its ear for sorrow

if not in its eye for significance,
given how levon helm's human heartbeat
had to held on so tight to time at his drum kit
despite carrying such a weight in his voice box,
while leonard cohen's gift with ghosts
still haunts every single secret chord
in hallejulah,
joined since by k d lang
in coverage so transcendent,
leaving joni mitchell to sit alone in a bar,
mapping canada by the north star
in a case of you,
whereas far to the south
bonnie raitt still opts not to slide
down a bottleneck as an angel
from montgomery
her man back home in the evening
with nothing to say,
while aretha franklin demands respect
for evermore as a soul sister
having spelt such things right out...
notwithstanding all of that
bob dylan
simply stands alone
beside his dove asleep in the sand,
the folk laureate of a lifetime
crafting a dozen or more
most lyric of songs
I've loved for so long...
just like you my sweet one

both our kids too,
each of you three adored
all through,
right down to my holey old socks
past darning,
keeping the better part of me
forever young

This first bookcase will soon turn fifty

A villanelle

Built with care at the age of fifteen
Back in a high school woodwork class
This first bookcase will soon turn fifty

Shelves duly set at paperback width
Varied in height in either half
Topped off with bookend flair at fifteen

Sharp in focus then, never drifting
Masking joinery, hiding art
In no case foreseen as reaching fifty

By breeze-borne seeds my youth uplifted
Poems like thistledown floating past
Drafted with care ever since fifteen

Volumes by voices far more gifted
Showing ways forward first to last
Housed in a bookcase bound for fifty

Here with half a century's shifting
Still raw at heart, hidden with art
Crafting with care since aged fifteen
Bookcase and verse both turning fifty

Thanks

Across a lengthy period of time, thanks to many people for supporting such work, including Ricky Allan, Clive & Sally Alsop, Kellie Asmussen, Penelope Asselineau, David Ballantyne, Marcus Barker, Donna Barnard, Edwin & Martine Batt, Sheree Beecher, John Black, Chris & Liz Borlace, Otto Boron, Mark Braddick, Lauren Bruce, Robyn Cairns, Iain Colquhoun, Todd Cook, Peter Cooke, Mel Crookston, Dee Crosby, Evan Curwood, Adrian Darakai, Guy Dimmick, Kate Driscoll, Naomi Duff, Birgit Eriksson, Jennifer Fell, Amelia Fielden, Lorin Ford, Bill Frew, Kay & Keely Frost, Beverley George, Nicola Greve, Alleyne Hall, Bella & Donna Hallam, Ewan Harris, Jeannie Haughton, Kris Hemensley, William Henderson, Paul Kane, Cherie Kilpatrick, Hedy & Peter Kirkbride, Ellen Koshland, Jai Law, Rosanna Licaria, Vincent Long, Janet Marsh, Laura McCarthy, James McCaughey, Jo McInerney, Kathy Meikle, Hayley Mott, Karen Mowat, Russell Moyle, Sue Murphy, Brett Niven, Meg O'Brien, Tegan O'Dea, Marge O'Donnell, Marlene Ogden, Kathie Olden, Anne & Ian Outhred, Danielle Payne, Patricia Prime, Daniel Printannier, Lorraine Proctor, Jane Refshauge, Corissa Rieschiek, Peter Roberts, Johanna & Norm Rough, Linton Rousseau, Cynthia Rowe, Yvette Stubbs, Gary Sullivan, Jill Thompson, Helen Timbury, Riccardo Velardi, Sally Walk, Steve Wiegerink, Bronwyn Williams, Leanne Williams, Pam Williams, Ricky Williams, Rohan Williams, Sophie Williams, Mark Wilson and Jo Wolswinkel; along with the late Paul Carter, Trevor Cox, Lisa Demos, Loretta Hemensley and Janet Williams.

CPSIA information can be obtained
at www.ICGtesting.com
Printed in the USA
LVHW080042191021
700772LV00013B/578

9 781761 091957